DEDICATION

This work is dedicated;
to my inestimable mother,
Mrs Jane E. Kalu

If you have purchased this book without a cover you should be aware that this book may have been stolen property and reported as "unsold and destroyed" to the publisher. In such case neither the author nor the publisher has received any payment for this "stripped book".

This publication is designed to provide competent and reliable information regarding the subject matter covered.

Not all scripture quotations were taken from the King James Version of the Bible. Please note that wherever "he" or "him" is used in the book to signify a child, it is always in a generic form; meaning both male and female child.

Copyright © 2014 by Stanley Ifeanyi Kalu
All right reserved. No part of this book may be copied or reproduced in any manner whatsoever without the written consent of the publisher or the Children Mentors, Inc.

MENTORING GOD'S HERITAGE

By

STANLEY IFEANYI KALU

Aba, Enyimba City

PRAISE FOR
MENTORING GOD'S HERITAGE

"This work, Mentoring God's Heritage, is a good, commendable and timely efforts by Stanley Ifeanyi Kalu to re-awaken our society particularly parents, families, leaders, teachers and adults alike to their civic responsibility, duty and assignment from God to bring up children; imperatively as role models, in godly manner and in effect, make them useful members of the society.

I adjudge it timely in the light of the increasing social ills, deteriorating moral standards, juvenile delinquency, and high rate of unruly, uncultured and ungodly behaviour including a dangerously increasing violent disposition by youths now unfortunately rampant and unhealthily prevalent in our present-day society.

Notwithstanding its un-broadened referencing; mainly centered on the most precious and valuable book – the Holy Bible, it is a veritable tool for parents, families, institutions, organisations, and the society in their quest to successfully mentor children as God's heritage.

I commend the author for this effort and recommend the work to all who are in position of mentoring children.

- Elder Obiefula Igwe Chukwu
  St Andrews Presbyterian Church of Nigeria
  First Aba Parish

"Stanley is really hitting the hammer at the head of the nail, based on the negligence of parents to the divine mandate on children. He offers the sort of advice which is hard to refuse.
- Pastor Mrs. Goodness M. Johnson
  Solid Faith Ministry International

ACKNOWLEDGMENTS

This work is a result of a lifetime of learning and development personally, and it is also the collective contribution of many mentors, teachers, supporters, advisors, friends, and family. I am continually cognizant of the fact that we are all the sum total of what we have learned, as well as the products of the contributions made by so many other people to our lives, as we journey to our ultimate destiny.

No achievement in life is without the help of many known and unkwown individuals who have impacted our lives. We owe every measure of our success to the array of input from so many. I would like to thank some great personalities whose words and actions have always leaved me better than they found me.

To Jane E. Kalu, for being a loving authoritarian and God's best for me;

To Okoro Okereke and Awa Eke Kalu; for their consistent discipline, counsel and excellent wisdom;

To Victor Iwo Mang, for laying the foundation of inspirational knowledge;

To Ifeanyi A. Uche; for being a respected and admired friend;

To P.C.M children and teachers, for your discernment and enthusiasm for my life;

To Boys' Brigade Nigeria, for your twenty-two years of training.

I want to specially thank Rev. Ikechukwu I. Nduka, Elder Dr. Joseph A. O. Anya, Elder Obiefula Igwe Chukwu, Mrs Goodness M. Johnson, and Chukwuemeka U. Kalu for their contributions, advice and corrections to this book.

This list would not be complete without thanking Rebecca Oluchi Ogbonna for typesetting the manuscript and the incredible team members of Children Mentors Inc for their empowerment.

Thank you.

TABLE OF CONTENTS

Introduction 13

CHAPTER 1
Training in God's image 18

CHAPTER 2
Is it Authoritarian or Permissive method? 33

CHAPTER 3
Consistency: Blessing for Obedience and Correction for Disobedience 43

CHAPTER 4
The Growing Child 55

CHAPTER 5
The Place of Discipline 79

CHAPTER 6
The Clarion Call 103

IN CONCLUSION
Your Child's Time Table 112

Endnotes 118

FOREWORD

A close look around us, one would discover that there is a general disorder and indiscipline among children. Children need love and personal attention, but many are not receiving it in the quantities they should have. The rate of divorce is on the increase in our society. As homes break up, children loose the benefit of resident father or mother. The remaining parent who usually must work has less time and energy to devote to active growing children who are going through trauma as a result of divorce.

Children need protection from this evil world; but today's children are exposed to doses of sex, violent and profanity. They see it on television, hear it on the radio and observe it in the lives of adults who have abandoned the traditional values which were once commonly held even by non-Christians.

Children are inheritance from God. Today, more than ever before, children need the attention, love and help of concern Christians and ministers who understand their deepest needs and who want to help these boys and girls experience the quality of life God intended for them to have. If the children of today do

not have their needs met; if they do not come to the saving knowledge of Christ and learn how to live and grow in Him, from whence will the church of tomorrow come?

Stanley Ifeanyi Kalu, the author of this book, "Mentoring God's Heritage", has gone through so many children training and has been teaching in the Presbyterian Children Ministry of Saint Andrews Presbyterian Church of Nigeria, First Aba Parish for the past ten years. He has exhibited in this book the importance of mentoring children so that we can have a better society tomorrow.

I therefore, sincerely recommend this book to anybody who would want to be part of the group of mentoring God's heritage.

- Rev. Ikechukwu I. Nduka
  Minister in Charge
  St Andrews Presbyterian Church of Nigeria
  First Aba Parish

FOREWORD

This book "Mentoring God's Heritage" is very timely, more especially as the dawn of each new day is characterised by a new system of violence that are caused by human elements, who by nature were not adequately instructed toward the Christian faith before the age of hostility. In other words, the problem of violence experienced world over stems from wrong foundation of the child's upbringing.

Stanley is positing that the key to directing children aright is through early purposeful instruction by parents. This is because the "home" remains the starting point for the child's mentoring. The instruction given at the early stage of the child's development will be very useful especially when the child "retain" those words of teaching.

In fact, the character or lifestyle our children will exhibit tomorrow depends immeasurably on what we put into them today.

The author, though young has acquired experiences through involvement in the children ministry, reading and of course in attending conferences, seminars, etc.

I sincerely recommend this book as a useful tool to every home, anyone that has the interest of the welfare of the growing child at heart, and teachers of all categories who are helping the children in their early development.

- Elder Dr. Joseph A. O. Anya
  **St Andrews Presbyterian Church of Nigeria
  First Aba Parish**

AUTHORS' NOTE

The Overview:

It has become a heart-rending moment on the continuous fall of the moral standard of our children. Parents' pattern of training their sons and daughters has become that of trial and error approach. The societies we live in have taken over the job of parenting. Our children have become a sponge currently soaking up whatever character they see along the way. Violence and sexual themes flood the media as never before, and peer pressure in the school system is ever present. Satan is constantly broadcasting as the "prince of the power of the air" (Ephesians 2:2), and he is ever ready and willing to influence our children. Who can remedy the situation? Even the supposed experts on mentoring children have strongly disagreed among themselves on the way to deal with these problems. And yet there aren't much written about God's practical direction and pattern on how to train His heritage (Psalm 127:3). This is a real pity because millions of parents, mentors of children, and everyone who has children under their care would love to read about this subject.

"MENTORING GOD'S HERITAGE" is a book that generally reveals God's practical guidelines on how to train his heritage, explaining the ways on how to handle the life of children and teenagers, and why the home is God's provision to nurture children.

INTRODUCTION

I think that maybe every mentor that wants to train a child in the way he should go, should be going that way because a child have never been very good at listening to their elders, but they have never failed to imitate them.
- *Stanley Ifeanyi Kalu*

If you have a child and a teenager under your control, or you are a parent, this book was written for you.

It represents many hours of children training experience that have been done over the past ten years at Presbyterian Children Ministry under St. Andrew's Presbyterian Church of Nigeria in Aba, Enyimba City, Abia State, Nigeria.

It illustrates the real purpose of monitoring God's heritage, as people ponders whether it was merely to bring up children to become independent and competent adults or whether there is something more to it. Read on for the amazing answer!

What we have discovered is that parents who are mentors of their children works far more than they should in training their children but they are not getting the required result.

Indeed, the problem is not that the parent doesn't train; the problem is they're giving the wrong training. As a result, most of their children end up with unrewarding, unpredictable, and unmanageable characters.

Why is this?

Why do so many mentors go into training, only to fail?

What lesson aren't they learning?

Why is it that with all the information available today on how to be successful in training God's children, so few people really are?

This book answers those questions.

"Mentoring God's Heritage" is all about bringing up God's inheritance according to His pattern and direction. Everyone was created for God and His purpose. So, mentoring God's Heritage is not about us (mentors), but it is all about God; for his inheritance to honour and acknowledge Him in their lives. We must therefore ask ourselves these questions:

Who is God's Heritage?

How does God want His heritage to be mentored? In other words, what is the responsibility placed on us as mentors of God's heritage?

What are the punishments of not mentoring God's heritage?

Ignore the answers to these questions and you will join the hundreds of thousands of parents who pour their energy, capital, and life into training their children and fail, or the many others who struggle through life simply trying to mentor a child.

What then can we really regard the training of a child to be?

The training of a child is like the bending of a rod. You can only bend a rod when you have heated it in a blacksmith forge. While it is still hot and reddish in colour that is the best time to bend to your desired shape and style. The bending takes time, needs your strength (energy) and application of force to actualize the desired shape. To bend the rod to the shape of a knife, you must be an expert. You must know the rules and procedures (knowledge) or you will miss the step, thereby producing a blunt knife which is useless and of no importance.

The training of a child can also be likened to the forming of the foundation of a building. Once the foundation is not strong, the building will collapse either during the process of construction or after many years of completing the construction. The collapse leads to the death of the occupants. The failure of the building is always due to the wrong choice and application of building materials, and failure to follow the engineer's standard specification. That is to say; the child that is left without a good training during his formative years may one day cause the death of his parents and so much heart breaks. The High Priest Eli is an example (1 Samuel 3:11-14).

What a child becomes in life is dependent on the type of training he/she receives. A child can also be likened to a sponge ready to soak up whatsoever it sees along the way.

These illustrations tell us that good home upbringing is very important in the lives of our children especially in their formative years. It helps them to develop a strong positive character. It also helps them to combine what they believe with character. Remember they fully learn from whatever they see us do.

Children are blessings from God. Are parents a blessing too? In this book, we are going to see how parents are a blessing to their children. How the home/family is God's special blessing and provision to nurture children. We will see the revelation of God's guidelines on how to train His children according to His pattern and direction, and also understand the battles in the life of teenagers.

Good reading.

1
TRAINING IN GOD'S IMAGE

*Children are living jewels dropped
unsustained from heaven.*
- *Robert Pollok*

Lo, children are an heritage of the LORD; and the fruit of the womb is his reward. As arrows are in the hand of a mighty man; so are children of the youth. Happy is the man that hath his quiver full of them: they shall not be ashamed, but they shall speak with the enemies in the gate" (Psalms 127:3-5).

Children are God's inheritance, you can even say children are God's birthright; they are His legacy and a gift from Him. God gives us children as a reward so that we will not be ashamed.

When a couple marries, the natural progression should be for them to begin to multiply and replenish the earth just as God commanded. This comes into fruition in each couple's lives at different times. A major challenge after having children is usually how to raise them. It will be a privilege if you participate in nurturing the future generation. It is an awesome responsibility to be chosen by God to mentor His heritage. He will ask us at the end how well we have obeyed His instructions.

Who is a mentor?

A mentor is a person of many parts and attributes. A mentor is an adviser, a counselor, a guide, a tutor, a teacher, a shepherd and a leader, all combined. In the home/family, parents are the mentors of their children.

Now that we know who a mentor is: what guidelines has God given us to mentor His heritage.

The Bible is full of instructions on the responsibilities of mentors, as well as that of a child to the mentor. The Bible gives us clear instructions on how God wants His heritage to be taken care of and to be mentored. In the Old Testament we hear of God blessing Abraham with these words,

> **"And I will make of thee a great nation, and I will bless thee, and make thy name great, and thou shall be a blessing. And I will bless them that bless thee, and curse him that curseth thee: and in thee shall all families of the earth be blessed" (Genesis 12:2-3).**

> **"Neither shall thy name any more be called Abram, but thy name shall be Abraham; for a father of many nations have I made thee" (Genesis 17:5)**

Why did God bless Abraham so much? The answer is found in Genesis 18:19;

> **"For I know him, that he will command his children and his household after him, and they shall keep the way of the Lord, to do justice and judgment that the Lord may bring upon Abraham that which he hath spoken of him."**

Two things we see here. God blessed Abraham with children. God placed his own heritage in the hand of Abraham, because God knew he will command his children and his household after him, and they shall keep the way of the Lord, to do justice and judgment, so that the Lord may bring upon Abraham that which he hath spoken of him, that is the other blessings. When we sing Abraham's blessings are mine… many are looking for physical and material blessings. Many fail to see that in nurturing their wards and students, that God is making us the fathers and mothers of many nations. Each student or child you mentored in the way of the Lord is a blessing, a privilege, a gift and a responsibility from God. God is counting each of us worthy and saying as He testified of Abraham! For I know _____ (write your own name), that you will command your children to keep the way of the Lord, to do justice and judgment.

We see in several verses in the Bible, the many times God stressed the responsibility of mentoring children!

> **"And that thou mayest tell in the ears of thy son, and of thy son's son, what things I have wrought in Egypt, and my signs which I have done among them; that ye may know how that I am the LORD" (Exodus 10:2).**

> **"And thou shalt teach them diligently unto thy children, and shalt talk of them when thou sittest in thine house, and when thou walkest by the way, and when thou liest down, and when thou risest up" (Deuteronomy 6:7).**

"And Moses commanded them, saying, At the end of every seven years, in the solemnity of the year of release, in the feast of tabernacles, when all Israel is come to appear before the LORD thy God in the place which he shall choose, thou shalt read this law before all Israel in their hearing. Gather the people together, men, and women, and children, and thy stranger that is within thy gates, that they may hear, and that they may learn, and fear the LORD your God, and observe to do all the words of this law: And that their children, which have not known anything, may hear, and learn to fear the LORD your God, as long as ye live in the land whither ye go

> **over Jordan to possess it"**
> **(Deuteronomy 31:10-13).**

As we can see, bringing up children is all about God, for the children to honour and acknowledge Him. We are admonished in Joel 1:3, not only to tell your children of God, but you should also let your children tell their children, and their children another generation. In the New Testament, we see how important children are to Jesus Christ. In Mark 9:37, whosoever shall receive one of such children in my name, receiveth me: and whosoever shall receive me, receiveth not me, but him that sent me. In Mark 10:13, we are told that He was very displeased with His disciples who rebuked those that brought children unto Him, and went on to say "forbid them not, to come unto me: for of such is the kingdom of heaven".

God's intent is to bring up godly children in his image, who will reign under Him as kings and priests with Jesus Christ on this earth: "And have made us kings and priests to our God; and we shall reign on the earth" (Revelation 5:10).

For mentors, the ultimate goal is to lay a foundation in their children's formative years, during the time they can easily be influenced, so they will always desire to fully seek God as their father. That is the goal, though mentors cannot force children to make the right decisions. Even God, our father, does not force us to make right decisions. He will lead us and direct us but He will not force us. The goal of training God's heritage is to help our children to desire to walk in the footsteps of their mentors who are living God's way of life, and who are walking in the footsteps of their heavenly father. As mentors, we need to develop our children's desire to follow God, not just emphasize our desire for them to follow God.

Some people were blessed to have mentors who were very consistent in training them. Not all have been privileged to experience a pattern of consistency in training during their formative years but we all experience the pattern of our heavenly father, who is totally consistent with us. We can clearly see from God's word that He operates on the "blessing for obedience and correction for disobedience" principle. If we follow this principle consistently in monitoring God's heritage, we lay the foundation for the future family of God.

Yes, our personal example is of the utmost importance! Children must see the real God through their mentor's eyes. Young children's perception of God is primarily developed by their mentors' example. We cannot hope to rear godly children if we, as mentors, are not genuine godly examples. If children see intolerance, hypocrisy, self-centeredness and frequent anger, they will not likely be attracted to their mentors' belief system. Instead, the authority figures in their youth will provoke a negative attitude toward God's authority later in life.

Mentors need to prove fully, in their present life experience, that God's way of life is of very high value and works for them! If we have not clearly demonstrated to our children that God's principles work for us, how can we ever convince them that God's law are worthwhile, and that the godly principles we teach are good for them? If you are thinking they supposed to know! You're wrong.

As important as our example is, however, it is only a part of the whole. Even if every one of us could become the "perfect mentor," our perfection would not guarantee a perfect outcome. The Bible clearly speaks of Eli as "the priest of the LORD" (1 Samuel 1:3), yet we know that God refused to force Eli to make the right decision. God taught Eli to live His way of life, yet the perfect mentor had children who chose to reject His example and teaching. Later God's priest (Eli) mentored two sons (Hophni and Phinihas) who became sons of Belial (idol). The Bible recorded that "the sin of the young men was very great before the LORD…" (1 Samuel 2:17)

So, do we have any hope of mentoring children who will commit their lives to God? We live in a world that is under the influence of the "god of this age" (2 Corinthians 4:4), the "prince of the power of the air, the spirit who now works in the sons of disobedience" (Ephesians 2:2). The entertainment media are saturated with the perverted mindset of Satan's way of life. The world's education system is increasing in the satanic theory of evolution, as well as a continual destruction of any sense of morality.

One of the fundamental keys in mentoring God's heritage is that we must actively be demonstrating to our children that God's way works for us! By the example of our own lives, we must be able to show our children that God's principles will bring joy to their lives far beyond what Satan's system has to offer.

> **"But the fruit of the spirit is love, joy, peace, longsuffering, kindness, goodness, faithfulness, gentleness, self-control..." (Galatians 5:22-23).**

If you ask people on the street whether they would like to have a life full of love, joy, and peace, truly they will say: "Yes!" But the problem is that the average person today does not recognize the principles of God as the "cause" that will bring the "effect" of a very stable and joyous life. This occurs primarily because the world has not been called to true Christianity; rather, it is exposed to a false "so-called" Christianity. We as mentors must expose our children to the truth of the Bible; not just in the truth (doctrine) we teach, but also in the truth we live. If children experience a mentor who gives unconditional love, has easy to understand rules that are consistently reinforced and genuinely displays the fruits of God's spirit, it will not be difficult for them to develop respect and obedience to God as they grow up.

Many people have accepted the satanic lie that God's way of life is a "waste of time". They think God restricts us from every pleasure, resulting in a dull life of suffering and self-denial. If this is our image of God, our children will in time notice our approach and it will become their image of God as well. If, instead, mentors are truly thankful for the great God, and grasp the tremendous blessing of understanding God's way of life (which defines what is harmful for us and what will bring an abundant life, emotionally, mentally, physically and spiritually), our children will internalize this instead.

Jesus Christ taught that the kingdom of Heaven is like an invitation to a wedding:

> **"The kingdom of heaven is like a certain king who arranged a marriage for his son, and sent out his servants to call those who were invited to the wedding; and they were not willing to come" (Matthew 22:2-3).**

As with any invitation, some individuals accept and some do not even bother to respond. To be "called" by God and to be "Invited" by God are one and the same.

This is the invitation the Apostle Peter was describing on the Day of Pentecost when he said:

> **"For the promise is to you and to your children, and to all who are afar off, as many as the Lord our God will call" (Acts 2:39).**

Here we see that God offers His gift of the Holy spirit not just to the "you" who heard Peter speaking on Pentecost, but also to those who are "your children" – the offspring of Christian mentors – and to those who "are afar off, as many as the Lord our God will call".

For all of these, the promise of receiving God's spirit is conditional upon seeking and experiencing genuine repentance through Jesus Christ. Clearly, though the children of Christian mentors have potential access to God (1 Corinthians 7:14), not all will seek Him (God).

Our goal as mentors, then, is to do the best job we can possibly do in turning our children's heart to their true father, the supreme God. We want to mold them as best we can, while we have the opportunity in their early years to lay a foundation for their future. Not every child will choose to go God's way fully, but our teaching and training will not be wasted! Knowledge of God's laws at least to the extent that they are followed will still benefit our children in their lives. This is true even for those whose mentors are not Christians. God's laws operate on cause and effect, and to the extent that even non-Christians apply the spiritual laws of God, they will have better lives.

And for those children who "see the light" in their youth and turn fully to their God, what an amazing future they have! God offers to be their mentor and their partner for life, guiding them through every decision and milestone in their life, just like a loving physical father. The result will be better marriages, stronger families, peaceful and stable mindsets.

So we mentors have a very high calling. Our God is training us as His children in His image! In turn, God is calling us to train and shape our children in His image. This is a very high goal in a dark and dangerous world. God being a loving mentor promises that:

> **"… I will never leave you nor forsake you. So we may boldly say: The Lord is my helper…" (Hebrews 13:5-6).**

The closer we move to our heavenly father through studying His word and putting them into practice, the more we will in our own lives emulate His qualities as the perfect mentor. Every last mentor has made mistakes in their training, but God knows that mentors, like their children, are capable of learning and changing.

Yes, this is easier said than done, but with God's guidance there is real hope.

As mentors, let us rededicate our lives to turning the hearts of the children to their heavenly father. This is the ultimate goal and purpose of having children: to "train them in God's image".

2

IS IT AUTHORITARIAN OR PERMISSIVE METHOD?

If you bungle raising your children, I don't think whatever else you do well matters very much.

- *Jacqueline Kennedy Onassis*

Why is training of children so difficult? One obvious answer is that it involves many things that may be different in different situations, so that you cannot be sure what will happen or predict the result accurately because many of them are beyond our control. Our primary examples in training children have been our own mentors. Whatever we have experienced from our mentors is the pattern that is permanently stamped on our minds, whether good or bad. The example we have experienced with our own mentors, of course, cannot be changed; the past is beyond our control. But none of us are prisoners of the past. With God's help, we can be victorious over the challenges of the present.

The society we live in also shapes and molds our children. Violence and sexual themes flood the media as never before, and peer pressure in the school system is ever present. Satan broadcasts constantly as the "prince of the power of the air" (Ephesians 2:2), and he is ever ready and willing to influence our children.

Even the supposed experts on monitoring children have strongly disagreed among themselves. Over many years we have seen wild swings of the pendulum among those who claim, to know the answers. Society has debated as to what is most important in child's training, whether it is developing self-control or self-esteem? Those who believe self-control is the primary value subscribe to what can be called the authoritarian method, where: the mentor's word is law, not to be questioned, and misconduct brings strict punishment. Authoritarian mentors seem unfriendly from their children, showing little love, caring and attention. Maturity demands are high, and mentor-child communication is rather low.

Of course, these traits are a mixture of good and bad. When misconduct brings consistent punishment, the demand for maturity is high. However, studies show that: "Children whose mentors are authoritarian are likely to be obedient but not happy and at the long run they tend to be rebellious".

In comparison to those who most value self-control, mentors who consider self-esteem the primary goal of training children tend to subscribe to the permissive method in which: "the mentors make few demands on their children, hiding any impatience they feel about them. Discipline is not strictly carried out. The mentors on this side are showing more love, caring and attention. They are accepting and communicating well with their children. They make few maturity demands because they view themselves as available to help their children but not as responsible for shaping how their offspring turn out".

Here, again, these traits are a mixture of both good and bad. Amazingly, studies show that: "those whose mentors are permissive are likely to be even less happy and lack self control.

So which is the most important goal in training children: is it developing self-esteem or self-control? Is the authoritarian or the permissive model the best method of training? When some mentors gave an answer to these questions, they tend to answer based on the style of training they have been using.

A similar question might be asked: when pouring a concrete foundation, which is more important, is it the cement powder composed of minerals, sand and rock, or the water that mixes into the powder?

In fact both are needed to make a strong lasting foundation. The proportions of water and powder must be properly balanced to have any lasting strength. Too much water and not enough cement will make a very weak foundation. Too much cement and too little water will produce a weak and crumbly foundation. Both are extremely important for lasting strength.

As you may well know, both self-control and self-esteem are equally essential for a child's lifelong well-being.

Children trained by authoritarian mentors grow up with a sense of never measuring up. They tend not to venture out of their limited comfort zone. Socially they are self-conscious, and they feel insecure and anxious. They grow into teens and adults who are always trying to prove themselves.

Children trained by more permissive mentors tend to have self-esteem, but lack self-control. For the rest of their lives, they become slaves to their immediate strong desire to do something without thinking about the consequences. They cannot sit still long enough to pay attention in the classroom. Succeeding in the university is difficult, and holding down a job for a long time may be equally difficult. Since they don't have self-control, they have difficulty tolerating situations that are not immediately pleasant to them.

Clearly, an imbalance in either self-esteem or self-control is a serious handicap for the rest of a child's life.

What every child needs is a balance of the two, which can be called "loving authority". This would consist of equal parts of self-esteem and self-control. Together, these will build a stronger foundation for a child, just as the right balance of cement powder and water bond together into the most stable concrete.

In this loving authority, mentors set limits and enforce rules, but they are also willing to listen respectfully to the child's requests and questions. They will make high maturity demands on their children, communicate well and also love and care for them.

When you think about it isn't this exactly the style of training that we find in the Bible? God sets limit for us, but He is ever willing to listen to us as we come to Him in prayer. He makes high maturity demands for our spiritual growth, but communicates with us through His written word, giving us equal amounts of encouragement and forgiveness.

The Importance of Building Self – Control

When children are given solid guidelines over which they cannot cross, those guidelines become internal restraints that we call "self – control". In children, self – control becomes the restraints which they exercised with fears, emotions and desires. When children cross over the guidelines and receive discipline, they learn that their actions have consequences. Well – disciplined children are a delight to their mentors, because they are not constantly trying to cross over the guideline.

God made this abundantly clear when He inspired the instruction to mentors:

> **"Correct thy son, and he shall give thee rest; yea, he shall give delight unto thy soul" (Proverbs 29:17)**

Firm guidelines and restrictions to children provide a measure of safety and security to them.

The Importance of Building Self – Esteem

Real love is unconditional. The Apostle Paul was inspired to write: "Love suffers long and is kind… bears all things… love never fails" (1 Corinthians 13:4, 7-8)

Unconditional love means loving your children, no matter what. No matter what the child looks like. No matter what his assets, liabilities and handicaps are. No matter how he acts.

If we make the huge mistake of only loving our children when they please us, we will train children who never feel that they "measure up". All children make mistakes, and when love is dependent on being "mistake free", they will forever feel like incompetent failures. In the same way, if God only loved us when we were praying, fasting, studying the Bible or helping someone else, we would be unloved most of the time. The Bible says:

> **"But God commendeth his love toward us in that while we were yet sinners, Christ died for us" (Romans 5:8).**

God loves us, even though we make our share of mistakes. Christ loved us and died for us, even while we were going the wrong way.

Many of us mentors really do love our children, but have not adequately communicated this to them. Children care more about how we act toward them, than about what we say or what we feel inside. So how can we show love to them in ways that they can readily understand and appreciate?

One vital tool is eye contact. Looking a child in the eyes in a loving manner says, loud and clear: "I value you, you are important to me". For children emotional well-being they need eye contact from their mentors. Children seem to look deeply into other people's eyes seeing their degree of sincerity and genuineness.

Physical contact is another vital tool needed to show love to children. Notice how Jesus Christ Himself interacted with young children:

> **"And they brought young children to him, that he should touch them: and his disciples rebuked those that brought them. But when Jesus saw it, He was much displeased and said unto them, suffer the little children to come unto me, ….. And He took them up in his arms, put his hands upon them, and blessed them" (Mark 10:13-14, 16).**

Appropriate physical contact is a life-long value between mentors and children. At any age, a hand on the shoulder, a pat on the back and an occasional hug are always possible.

Undivided attention is also vital. Undivided focused attention means giving your children full, undivided attention in such a way that he feels truly loved, that he knows he is so valuable in his own right that he wants your watchfulness, appreciation, and uncompromising regard.

If you did not show your children love during their formative years, please don't expect too much attention from them during your old age as they do not know much about it because you didn't train them on it.

So back to the question: which is more important in monitoring God's heritage: is it authoritarian or permissive method? Both are absolutely necessary.

Children who receive unconditional love, and are taught obedience through loving authority, have the greatest likelihood of success in life. Authority without unconditional love invariably brings anger and rebellion. When the proper balance is applied, God's summary of obedience and self – discipline can be realized:

> **"Children, obey your parents in the Lord, for this is right….. And, ye fathers, provoke not your children to wrath: but bring them up in the nurture and admonition of the Lord" (Ephesians 6:1,4).**

3
CONSISTENCY: BLESSING FOR OBEDIENCE AND CORRECTION FOR DISOBEDIENCE

Children are unpredictable. You never know what inconsistency they're going to catch you in next.
- *Franklin P. Jones*

God is totally consistent in how He deals with us, His children. His guidelines are always valid, and His word is totally trustworthy. He does not violate His own law.

God tells us: "For I am the Lord, I do not change" (Malachi 3:6). This means that God is consistent in His laws, His spiritual principles and His ways of life.

We often see the fruit of inconsistency in the daily lives of people around us. For example: we might have seen a mother who yelled out in extreme frustration to her children to stop running up and down. They would calm down for a moment or two, and they would take off again. After a few minutes, the mother would yell out. "Do you want me to whip you?"

This yelling, screaming, inconsistent mother made her life miserable! Her children always knew that if they slowed down for a few moments, their mother's wild and irresponsible threats would subside, and they could soon go back to what they were doing. This is an act of inconsistency in a child's training and shouldn't be so.

Consistency in discipline is extremely important because everything else depends on it. Christ taught His disciples; He encouraged them, and sometimes corrected them. His goal was to train disciples who could live and teach the way of life.

Mentors should discipline their children with encouragement, praise and rewards, and also with correction and penalties. This is the same principle that God uses with us. He promises us blessings for obedience (Deuteronomy 28:1-14) and correction or penalties for disobedience (Deuteronomy 28:15-46).

The dictionary defines "Consistency" as "the quality of always being the same, doing things in the same way, having the same standards" (Longman Dictionary of Contemporary English). Another dictionary defines "Consistency" as "constant, steady, regular, persistent, unchanging, undeviating, unified" (Webster's

Seventh New collegiate Dictionary). That describes the type of mentor that anyone would want, especially when accompanied by a healthy dose of unconditional love and appropriate forgiveness. This is a fertile ground for a child's healthy growth, along with having a sense of being valued and the security of firm guidelines that will not change.

Regrettably, many mentors have tried to rework the creator's child training principles into whatever seems best to them. Without realizing, that they are acting as though they know more about child training than God Himself does.

Some years ago, many mentors relied primarily on restrictive authority and on punishment for disobedience. Little unconditional love was given, and mentors with this approach became unloving authoritarians. In recent years, the pendulum has swing in the opposite direction, with mentors offering more than enough praise and encouragement, but little or no correction or discipline for disobedience.

So, what can we say about this; being consistently authoritarian is not the answer! Being consistently permissive is not the answer! True consistency requires the balance that we find in God's word – which includes real blessings for obedience, and penalties for disobedience.

Consistent penalties for disobedience teach children a lesson that will benefit them for their entire lives – the lesson of "cause and effect". This is how the world operates. If you jump out from three-storey building, gravity will always work, and you will pay the price for your mistake. Break the laws of the land, and there is a price to pay. Transgress God's instructions, and there is always a price to pay. Children need to live in a family environment where they know that if they violate the mentors' rules or standards of behaviour, there is always a price to pay.

Mentors who do not teach their children "cause and effect" do their children a serious disservice. How can a child learn cause and effect if he never experiences the effect of his behaviour? How can a very young child who is just learning to walk learn cause and effect if, when he is told to "come here", he ignores his father without any follow-up discipline? How can a young child learn cause and effect if he behaves very angrily and unreasonably in front of his mother especially when he can't have the toy he wants and she simply shrugs her shoulders or sigh in annoyance? How can a teenager learn cause and effect if he receives a bill for breaking glasses in school and his mentors pay the fine without any follow-up discipline?

Consistency with a very young child who is just learning to walk, with rules and guidelines and punishment for disobedience, leads to consistency as a teen, which leads to consistency as an adult, which can lead to consistency as a future son of God. The process of learning cause and effect – with consistent blessings for obedience and correction for disobedience – is the foundation for future character formation and for a successful life. Mentors can either assist God with this process, or make the eventual conversion process more difficult for their children.

> **"Because sentence against an evil work is not executed speedily, therefore the heart of the sons of men is fully set in them to do evil" (Ecclesiastes 8:11).**

The pattern that is set in childhood generally carries on through life. A mentor who does not consistently discipline quickly for disobedience does not establish the "cause and effect" principle in a child's early years. The resulting child, teen and adult sees rules and guidelines (whether in the home or in the school system or on the job) as restrictions that only occasionally bring negative consequences. The word of God tells us that:

> **"Now no chastening for the present seemeth to be joyous, but grievous: nevertheless afterward it yieldeth the peaceable fruit of righteousness unto them which are exercised thereby" (Hebrew 12:11).**

How peaceful it is when children have been taught obedience right from the start. Even young children can be a real joy to a family when they are taught the habit of obedience.

When a child is old enough to be taught to "come" when called, there are never any exceptions to obedience. For example, you might have seen some mentors actually counting: "1, 2, 3, . ." and when the child does not come, the mentor may finally walk over to the child and pull him by the hand. This becomes an early lesson to the child on how he can control his mentors.

Another popular threat is: "I'm telling you for the last time. "Even this threat may become: "This is your last … last chance".

Many mentors tell their children, over and over again, to "do something" or to "stop doing something". Finally, they explode in anger when they cannot tolerate their children's disobedience any longer. This teaches a child that "cause and effect" only applies when mentors become very annoyed and upset, and that the "trick" for a child is to learn to read the signs of when mentors are coming close to their limit.

Mentors make it so much easier on themselves when they teach their children that "no" means "no" and "yes" means "yes". Life is much more difficult for mentors when they allow whining and pleading to occur. When mentors give in to such pleas, they teach their children an important lesson: if they whine and plead long enough, the mentor will eventually give in, and they get what they want.

Every mentor who has disciplined a child has likely found at times that the child was crying not from sorrow or repentance, but from obvious anger. Anger is like a "muscle" – the more it is exercised, the more it will develop. If a child's anger is not addressed, the necessary lesson will not be learned – and nothing will be gained but a hardening of the child's attitude. In this circumstance, it becomes necessary to remind the child why he was disciplined in the first place, and then explain that he will also be disciplined for his attitude of anger. In most cases, the child's attitude will change quickly, and his cry will turn more to a repentant spirit than to rebellion or anger.

As children are taught the principle of cause and effect: "blessing for obedience and punishment for disobedient", it is important that we do not forget the "blessing for obedience" side of the equation. Verbal approval for a job well done, including a greater level of eye contact and a smile, can accomplish a great deal. Children, like adults, appreciate being appreciated. We need to follow the example of God Almighty who promises to reward those who seek Him.

> **"... for he that cometh to God must believe that he is, and that he is a rewarder of them that diligently seek Him" (Hebrew 11:6).**

Mentors can also use gift as a reward for a job well done, including some allowance (money) for them to spend or save, after their tithe to God has been set aside. Yes, it is true that children should not be paid for routine obedience, such as coming when called or playing nicely with their brothers and sisters without fighting. But teaching children the value of the work ethic with rewards is certainly a right principle. Giving children an allowance without expecting anything in return is the wrong principle. Even God promises to reward us for our efforts:

> **"For the son of man should come in the glory of his father with his angels; and then he shall reward every man according to his works" (Matthew 16:27).**

Are we wiser at mentoring God's heritage than God the father Himself?

The sooner we ingrain in our young children the overall principle of consistent blessing for obedience and correction for disobedience, the more obedient a child becomes – and the more peaceful a household becomes. Consistency is a tremendous key! If you punish your child for a particular misbehavior today and ignore it tomorrow, you throw him into confusion at first. Then, if this becomes a trend, your child is made to believe that some bad behaviour is allowed. If this continues for a long time, it will become almost impossible to set that child straight. It is very important that there is consistency in disciplining your child.

We must remember that children, since they have human nature, are attracted to disobedience like a magnet - and disobedience must be dealt with consistently. On the other hand, obedience and doing what is right must be taught.

> **"Train up a child in the way he should go: and when he is old, he will not depart from it" (Proverbs 22:6).**

Every rule or guideline should be logical and explainable. Instead of just telling a child "don't run into the street", you can add "I don't want you to be injured or hit by a car".

The fundamental purpose of any discipline must be the child's well-being! The underlying reason for discipline should never be anger. Most mentors have probably, at some time lashed out in anger when frustrated or very annoyed or upset. This is something that we must all work to overcome. Remember God's instruction:

> **"And, ye fathers, provoke not your children to wrath: but bring them up in the nurture and admonition of the Lord"** (Ephesians 6:4).

Children must learn and know that we discipline them because we love them. We really do want what is best for them, and we want them to grow up to be happy and successful adults as well as fulfilled members of the family of God.

How important it is that we begin to teach our children today, no matter what their age, the vital lesson of "cause and effect" – blessing for obedience and correction for disobedience. This is the foundation for their eventual eternal life.

> **"I call heaven and earth to record this day against you, that I have set before you life and death, blessing and cursing: therefore choose life, that both <u>thou</u> and thy <u>seed</u> may live"** (Deuteronomy 30:19).

This is God's principle of training His heritage as sons of God. It should also be our principle of training our own children, for their life – long happiness.

4
THE GROWING CHILD

You are the bows from which your children, as living arrows, are sent forth.

- *Kahlil Gibran*

Many things in life can wait, but child growth and training cannot. A child can't wait. Every child needs his mentor. He needs the mentor's time, affection, attention, guidance and heaven-imparted wisdom to enjoy a blissful relationship with his creator here on earth. It is important to train our children to be responsible; this is because a child that is trustworthy, dependable, competent and reliable tends to have a well-developed sense of self-worth. Such a child is a prime candidate for usefulness to God who is looking for faithful men and women He will entrust with responsibilities in His household (2 Timothy 2:2).

Training affects children's attitudes, actions and practical contribution to the family. We unwittingly court frustration, and lose our children to outside influences, when we allow our relationships, career and personal struggles to have a stranglehold on us. Allowing such distractions make children drift slowly into the world.

Most baby animals are self-supporting within few weeks of existence. This isn't the case with humans. It is natural for children to be in the home of, and somewhat dependent upon their mentors for support till adulthood. Interestingly, animal parents instinctively train their little ones; they chastise them, and teach them obedience and safe habits. Mother birds peck their baby chicks and nestlings; cows kick their calves to stop their over-boisterous attempts to get milk, and bears cuff their cubs vigorously sometimes, to stop a flight. All animal trainers and horsemen know that punishment is sometimes necessary in handling animals. Children are more precious than animals. They must be given the needed training, discipline, and correction to prepare them for a bright future.

Every mentor that appreciates his precious, charming, adorable and lovable child must understand that the same child, like every other human being, has inherent sinful tendencies, which, if not curbed, can lead to the child having an ingrained defiance to authority of any sort, including that of God. Mentors have to set boundaries for their children. Children, at every stage of their development, must be made to know the boundary between acceptable and unacceptable behaviour. They must be brought under strong, godly influence of their mentors, who harness their capabilities and potentials, so that they can become useful in every facet of life – to the family, the church and the society at large. God's command to every mentor is

Train up a child in the way he should go: and when he is old, he will not depart from it" (Prover22:6).

Newborns and Infants (0 – 12 months)

Mentoring newborns and infants is where the responsibilities of parenthood begin. A newborn's basic needs are food, sleep, comfort and cleaning, which the mentor provides. An infant's only communication is crying, and attentive mentors will begin to recognize different needs such as hunger, discomfort, loneliness. Newborns and young infants require feedings every few hours, which is disruptive to adult sleep circles. They respond enthusiastically to soft stroking, cuddling and caressing. Gentle rocking back and forth often calms a crying infant, as do massages and warm baths. Newborns may comfort themselves by sucking their thumbs or a pacifier. The need to suckle is instinctive and allows newborns to feed. Breast feeding is the best and recommended method of feeding. All major infant health organisations recommend six months exclusive breastfeeding of young infants.

From age 4 to 6 months, your infant can clearly recognize you and others who carry and care for him; especially siblings, friends, etc. He can also sit, though needs to be monitored closely, so he doesn't fall down. At this stage, you should sing and speak more to him with a cheerful countenance. Also, let him be with you during family devotions, listening to your hymns, Bible readings, and prayers.

And when he begins to crawl or walk (some early starters walk at 7 months), you should prevent him from going near electric sockets and refrigerators, touching naked wires, dipping hand in hot water, and walking on slippery floor. Also, keep away from his reach, dangerous objects such as chemicals, knives, razors, rolling objects and heavy loads that can easily fall over.

The forming of attachments is considered to be the foundation of the infant's capacity to form and conduct relationships throughout life. *Attachment* is the emotional bond which babies have with their mentors. Studies have shown that infants with secure attachment have the ability to form successful relationships, express themselves on an interpersonal basis and have higher self-esteem; while those without it exhibit behavioral problems such as disobedience, hostility and defiance towards authority figures.

Toddlers (1-3 years)

Toddlers are much more active than infants, and are challenged with learning how to do simple tasks by themselves. At this stage, you should be heavily involved in showing the child how to do things rather than just doing things for them. They also talk clearly than infants, and mimic a lot. Toddlers need help to build their vocabulary, increase their communication skills, and manage their emotions. Also, they'll begin to understand social etiquette such as politeness and taking turns.

Toddlers are very curious about the world around them, and are eager to explore it. They seek greater independence and responsibility, and may become frustrated when things don't go the way they want or expect. You should help guide and teach your toddler, and establish routines (such as washing hands before meals or brushing teeth before bed), as well as increase his responsibilities.

Your toddler is capable of memorising short verses of Scriptures and singing hymns. So, teach him. He also loves stories. Story telling is so important in teaching him Bible doctrines. Teach him to pray and praise God for dad, mum, siblings, food, friends, etc. Give him bright coloured toys; these interest toddlers much.

Children of this age bracket can genuinely be born again. Catherine Booth, wife of General Booth of the Salvation Army, testified that all her children were born again by the age of 3.

You too can lead your toddler to the new birth experience.

Teach him politeness, such as saying "OK," "Mum," "Thank you," "Excuse me, please" and "I'm sorry." You should also make him run simple errands like carrying your bag, and putting items in appropriate places.

Young Children (3-10 years)

Younger children are becoming more independent and beginning to build friendships. They are able to reason, and make their own decisions given hypothetical situations. They are very inquisitive too. Young children demand constant attention, but will learn how to deal with loneliness, and be able to play independently. They also enjoy helping and feeling useful and able. You should assist them by encouraging social interaction, and modeling proper social and moral behaviours.

At least 75 percent of a child's adult moral, intellectual and emotional traits are formed at the age of 6. This is also the great age of accountability. From ages 6 to 10 years, the child is gender conscious, and may dislike parents, siblings, relatives and other caregivers intruding into his privacy, especially when bathing or undressing. This is the age when he develops very fast morally, emotionally, psychologically and spiritually.

A large part of learning in the early years comes from being involved in activities and household duties. You should involve your children, especially the girls, in cooking and upkeep of the home. Teach them health, hygiene and eating habits through instruction and by example. You are expected to make decisions about their education too. Be heavily involved in arranging organised activities and early learning programmes for them.

Pre-teens (11-12 years)

Pre-teens experience rapid and irregular physical growth. They undergo bodily changes which are more visible in the physiology of girls than boys. The girls' maturity rate is also higher than the boys' at this stage. Hormonal changes in them cause them to be restless, and always wanting to do something that'll keep them busy. This is also the age of puberty.

As a caring mentor and adult, you should understand that your pre-teens' concern with their bodily changes accompanied by sexual maturation affects them emotionally, resulting in their unpredictability. This, coupled with peer pressures, makes mentoring at this stage the more challenging. Pre-teens need lots of love, caring, understanding and availability of authority figures.

Moreover, pre-teens learn responsibility and consequences of their actions, even without mentor's assistance. Therefore, use this period to help teach them the value of money, how to be responsible with it; be consistent and fair with their discipline; openly communicate with them, and do not neglect their needs. Be mindful of the friends they keep, the places they go, the books they read, the music they listen to and the programmes they watch on the television. Lead them to receiving Christian experiences of the New Birth, Sanctification and Baptism with the Holy Spirit, and encourage them to share their experiences with others.

Being the mentor of a pre-teen is not as scary as most people see it. Your pre-teens have just reached puberty, and are faced with many battles - the battle to be independent and to fit in a school, at home and among friends. It is your responsibility to help them with these battles, and ensure that they fit into their world just right. Keep in mind that helping your pre-teen to become an adult takes time, patience and commitment. Teens who are neglected or have too many conflicts with their mentors often connect with friends who tend to be anti-education and anti-social. Getting love, attention, respect and encouragement in the family helps teens to be less dependent on peer approval. There is no such thing as an instant adult. There are two things to remember here: (1) pre-teens need lots of love, and (2) they need a caring adult to show them right from wrong.

According to an expert, below are the various developments in pre-teen.

Intellectual Development
Your pre-teens
✓ Display a wide range of individual intellectual development
✓ Are in a transition period from concrete thinking to abstract thinking.
✓ Are intensely curious and have a wide range of intellectual pursuits, few of which are sustained.
✓ Prefer active over passive learning experiences.
✓ Prefer interaction with peers during learning activities
✓ Respond positively to opportunities to participate in real life situations.
✓ Are often preoccupied with self.
✓ Have a strong need for approval and may be easily discouraged.

✓ Develop an increasingly better understanding of personal abilities

✓ Are inquisitive about adults, often challenging their authority and always observing them

✓ May show disinterest in conventional academic subjects, but are intellectually curious about the world and themselves

✓ Are developing a capacity to understand higher levels of humour

Moral development
Yours pre-teens

✓ Are generally idealistic, desiring to make the world a better place and to become socially useful.

✓ Are in transition from moral reasoning which focuses on " what's in it for me" to that which considers the feelings and rights of others

✓ Often show compassion for those who are downtrodden or suffering, and have special concern for animals and the environmental problems that our world faces.

✓ Are moving from acceptance of adult moral judgments to development of their own personal values; nevertheless, they tend to embrace values consonant with those of their mentors.

✓ Rely on mentors and significant adults for advice when facing major decisions.

- ✓ Increasingly assess moral matters in shades of grey as opposed to viewing them in black and white.
- ✓ At times are quick to see flaws in others, but slow to acknowledge their own faults.
- ✓ Owing to their lack of experience, they are often impatient with the pace of change, underestimating the difficulties in making desired social changes.
- ✓ Value direct experience in participatory democracy.
- ✓ Greatly need and are influenced by adult role models who will listen to them and affirm their moral consciousness and actions as being trustworthy role models.
- ✓ Are increasingly aware of and concerned about inconsistencies between values exhibited by adults and the conditions they see in society.

Physical Development
Your pre-teens
- ✓ Experience rapid, irregular physical growth.
- ✓ Undergo bodily changes that may cause awkward, uncoordinated movements.
- ✓ Have varying maturity rates, with girls tending to mature one and half to two years earlier than boys.
- ✓ May be at a disadvantage because of varied rates of maturity that may require the understanding of caring adults.

✓ Experience restlessness and fatigue due to hormonal changes.

✓ Need daily physical activity because of increased energy.

✓ Develop sexual awareness that increases as secondary sex characteristics begin to appear.

✓ Are concerned with bodily changes that accompany sexual maturation and changes resulting in an increase in nose size, protruding ears, long arms, and awkward posture.

✓ Have preference for junk foods but need good nutrition.

✓ Often lack physical fitness, with poor levels of endurance, strength and flexibility.

✓ Are physically vulnerable because they may adopt poor health habits or engage in risky experimentation with drugs and sex.

Emotional Development

Your pre-teens

✓ Experience mood swings often with peaks of intensity and unpredictability.

✓ Need to release energy, often resulting in sudden, apparently meaningless outbursts of activity.

✓ Seek to become increasingly independent, searching for adult identity and acceptance.

✓ Are increasingly concerned about peer acceptance.

✓ Tend to be self-conscious, lacking in self-esteem, and highly sensitive to personal criticism.

✓ Exhibit intense concern about physical growth and maturity as profound physical changes occur.

✓ Increasingly behave in ways associated with their sex as sex role identification strengthens.

✓ Are concerned with many major societal issues as personal value systems develop.

✓ Believe that personal problems, feelings and experiences are unique to themselves.

✓ Are psychologically vulnerable, because at no other stage in development are they more likely to encounter so many differences between themselves and others.

Social Development

Your pre-teens

✓ Have a strong need to belong to a group with peer approval becoming more important as adult approval decreases in importance. In their search for self-actualization, they model behaviour after older, esteemed students or non-parents adults.

✓ May exhibit immature behaviour because their social skills frequently lag behind their mental and physical maturity.

✓ Experiment with new slangs and behaviours as they search for a social position within their group, often discarding these "new identities" at a later time".

- ✓ Are dependent on mentors' beliefs and values but seek to make their own decisions.
- ✓ Are often intimidated and frightened by their first middle level school experience because of the large numbers of students and teachers and the size of the building.
- ✓ Desire recognition for their efforts and achievements.
- ✓ Like fads, especially those shunned by adults.
- ✓ Often overreact to ridicule, embarrassment and rejection.
- ✓ Are socially vulnerable because, as they develop their beliefs, attitudes and values, the influence of media and negative experiences with adults and peers may compromise their ideals and values.

Adolescents (13-19 years) Mostly known as Teenagers

During this stage, children are beginning to form their identity, and are testing and developing the interpersonal and occupational roles that they will assume as adults. Therefore, it is important at this age that you treat them as young adults. Although teenagers look to peers and adults outside of the family for guidance and models for how to behave, mentors remain influential in their development.

Teenagers tend to increase the amount of time they spend with the opposite gender peers. However, they still maintain the amount of time they spend with the same gender, and they do this by decreasing the amount of time they spend with their mentors. Also, peer pressure is not just the reason why teenagers are influenced by peers, but because they respect, admire and like their peers. So, advising them to make godly friends and teaching them on how to identify one, is of great importance at this stage.

Mentors often feel isolated and alone in mentoring teenagers, but they should make efforts to be aware of their teenagers' activities, provide guidance, directions and consultation, because a child left to himself without positive mentors influence is a danger to himself, his family and the society at large. Mentoring issues at this stage of training include dealing with "rebellious" teenagers, who didn't know freedom while they were smaller. To tackle this problem, you must build a trusting relationship with them. When a trusting relationship is built, your teenagers are more likely to approach you for help when faced with negative peer pressure. Also, build up their self-esteem by building a strong foundation to help them resist negative peer pressure.

You should understand that adolescence is a paradox. The teenager is in-between a young child and an adult. He can choose to be either, and wants to be regarded that way by everybody, including his mentors. Hormonal changes in teenagers often make them unpredictable in response to situations. Though they are hero worshippers, they dislike hypocrisy, and can easily detect falsehood. They are sensitive to home conditions, and may become wayward if mentors often fight, and there's no show of love in the home.

Let your teenage child always attend religious meetings of godly teenagers, who will impact more on their lifestyles. Also, don't fail to discipline when necessary, *"**withhold not correction from the child: for if thou beatest him with the rod, he shall not die**"* (Proverbs 23:13).

Adults (20 upward)

Mentoring a child doesn't usually end when a child turns 19. Support can be needed in a child's life well beyond the teenage years, and continues into middle and later adulthood. Mentoring can be a lifelong process. You should understand that your role as an adviser, a guardian, teacher, shepherd, a leader, caregiver, protector, provider, counselor, encourager and disciplinarian doesn't stop as long as the child still lives under your roof. Even when far away from you, you have a responsibility to check on him. You must set limits and boundaries for your children, and make them live by them. Of course, you don't shove these down their throats, but by prayer, diligence, conscious and constant efforts, teaching and personal example, you will impact their future for good. Parental involvement has consistently been shown to exert the most influence over a child's success in every facet of life. So, you must do and give everything to raise your children in the fear and admonition of God. God will help you to succeed in Jesus' name!

Ten Qualities of Successful Mentors to a Growing Child

There is no responsibility greater than that of being a mentor to a growing child. Successful mentoring of God's heritage requires more than providing for the physical needs of one's children – it means being committed to their developmental well – being and

overall success. A goal of this magnitude requires mentors to give of themselves every day. Successful mentors are those who lift their children to heights they may never attain themselves. The qualities are here with for you to consume:

1. **Identify good qualities in your children.**

    Make a conscious effort to identify and compliment your children for their good qualities. Sometimes it is necessary to take a pause from the rush of life and enjoy the wonderful qualities that your children possess. Don't think for a moment that a mental note is enough. Point out your children's good qualities and let them build upon them.

2. **Make time daily to spend with your children.**

    Life has a way of consuming all of your time. It is easy to become "too busy" to do anything with your children. If you can't find the time, make the time. No matter how busy you are, or how tired you may be; there is no reason to deny your children of thirty minutes of your daily time. Give your children thirty minutes every day for whatever they wish to do.

3. **Communicate positively with your children.**

    Talk to your children in a positive way. Talk to them in a friendly manner about whatever subject they wish to discuss. Avoid falling into the trap of speaking to your children only when you need to discipline them.

Children get your attention most easily when they are getting into trouble, but don't make this the only time to talk to them because your speech will be less than pleasant. Give your children the benefit of positive communication and they will be more likely to talk to you in good times and bad.

4. **Involve children in household activities and family trips.**

Don't allow your children to become isolated in some remote corner of the house. It is important to allow your children a reasonable amount of privacy, but don't encourage them to become someone who chooses to live alone in their rooms.

Although this will be a subject of controversy, I would suggest keeping as many toys in one area of your home. Keep televisions, computers, and phones out of children's rooms whenever possible. Additionally the daily time allowed to use this attention demanding items should be regulated. Encourage family time and whenever possible do the unthinkable… talk to each other.

In addition to household activities, plan fun events outside of the house in which the children can be involved. Plan simple, but exciting activities that everyone can enjoy. You can also plan vacations and trips together when possible. Allow your children to contribute their ideas for your times together. Make a habit of giving the children something to look forward to with the family.

5. **Listen attentively to your children.**

    Be aware of the way you listen to your children – especially when you are busy. Take care to assure your children that you think that what they say is important. At times when you are preoccupied, it is easy to make the mistake of answering your children without paying full attention to what they are saying. When you find yourself answering your children by saying "uh huh", "yeah", or a similar manner of thoughtless speech, take note of it and pay closer attention to your children. As a mentor, you should surely take offense if your children answered you in this way. Be sure to look at them when they are talking to you. This may take a little extra effort, but it will make you give them the attention they deserve, and your children will see that you believe what they say is important.

6. **Be willing to change.**

    Part of your being a successful mentor is knowing when to change something about yourself. Everyone wants to be a perfect mentor, but there truly is no such thing. Mentors do make mistakes from time to time. There is nothing wrong with making mistakes as a mentor, as long as you can admit it to yourself and make changes for the better.

7. **Protect your children's safety.**

    Caring for the safety of your children may seem to be so obvious that it does not need mention. It is amazing how many mentors fail to care for even basic elements of their children's safety. From mentors who call upon their young children to cross a busy street after school while they sit in their cars, to others who let their children roam the streets without any knowledge of where they are, it can be disturbing to see how some mentors deprive their children of basic safety. Never gamble on the safety of your children.

8. **Do not allow your children to disrespect you or your spouse.**

   Being a good mentor does not mean you must allow your children to disrespect you or your spouse (partner). Be certain that your children understand what you expect of them in regard to respect.

9. **Don't argue with your spouse in front of the children.**

   In heated moments, this may seem difficult to avoid; but there is nothing that can be gained from arguing in front of your children. When something becomes a big enough issue that an argument is unavoidable, be aware that the children are watching and find a way to bottle it up and discuss it in private. There is nothing wrong with your spouse (or partner), but unless you want your children to be part of the argument, it is best to take care of the disagreement privately. Don't put children in a position where they will take sides or hear utterances that will be apologized for later. Whatever it takes keep your children out of your arguments.

10. **Tell your children you love them.**

Never refrain from telling your children you love them. Ignore any thoughts in your head that tell you not to do so. It is difficult to tell your children you love them too much, but it is easy to tell them too little. Don't let such a simple thing be a cause of regret. Tell your children you love them.

5
THE PLACE OF DISCIPLINE

True freedom is impossible without a mind made free by discipline.

- *Mortimer J. Adler*

Discipline means training, especially of the mind and character, aimed at producing self-control, obedience, etc. A necessary part of child training is discipline; it is what completes and makes it effective. There is a way to train up a child, and discipline is a part of that way.

Susana Wesley, who lived two centuries ago and turned out two of that generation's most dedicated ministers – Charles and John Wesley (as well as nine other children), had an interesting philosophy on rearing children:

> **The child who refuses to go to bed at night is the same that refuses to learn scriptures and follow the Lord. And just as surely as I'd see that child go to bed, I'd see that child come to God.**

To refuse to discipline your child is to prepare him for destruction. That was how Phinehas and Hophni, the two sons of Eli were destroyed. Their father refused to discipline them. He knew about their immorality, yet he refused to restrain them (1 Samuel 3:13).

Eventually, Eli was also destroyed. So, if you don't want God to destroy you, make sure you discipline your children. Therefore, child training is a responsibility of mentors (both father and mother), and discipline is a necessary part of the training.

It is very important to identify at what stage in a child's life to start instilling discipline. More often than not, that poses a challenge to a lot of parents who tend to believe that the child is still a child and knows nothing so disciplining should be postponed for when he is old enough to understand his actions.

As soon as a child is born, he is very active to absorb all the sights, sounds, and sensations that surround him. A baby's brain has been called "The most powerful learning machine in the universe". He is aware of his environment and is able to communicate. This type of communication is made evident when the baby cries for either food or a change of diaper, which the mother responds to. At times, the baby still continues to cry after a meal or diaper change. The baby is trying to communicate that there is some other thing amiss. In his view, he is the monarch of an empire populated by big people who were put here to serve him. The baby then begins to grow a set of teeth and what other way to run a test than on the mother's breast! It is instructive to note that mothers have different ways of registering their displeasure. For some, it is a reflex shout of pain. For others, it is taking the breast away from the baby for that moment. However, whichever method is employed, the baby gets the message and does not bite anymore. That is a form of registering displeasure.

As the child continues to grow, he may begin to assert himself. He may try to get his way all the time because his monarchy has been overthrown, and he may not take well to the new regime. Frustrated, he attempts to hold his ground. How? He may fall on the floor and kick his legs in the air, slap people's (especially mother's) face, cry uncontrollably. This is the time for you not to give in to any of his demands. At this age; discipline means putting clear, consistent limits on your child's behaviour and identifying misbehavior with a firm "no" or a negative expression. He will test you often so you must be prepared. No matter how loudly he cries, it will do the child no harm (it will probably strengthen the lungs). Remember, discipline means teaching, so teach your child the acceptable rules of life and existence clearly and consistently.

You may also introduce "two fingers". These two fingers can be used at the back of his palm as gentle as possible. The idea is not to inflict pain but to register your displeasure. You may thereafter in about five minutes, pacify the child by giving him a hug. You will have succeeded in letting the child know that though you love him, you will not be manipulated.

These are the formative years. By the time a child is nine years, he has already formed the character to build on for the rest of his life. At this stage in a child's life, you as a mentor will have to be very vigilant. Watch out for greed, selfishness, anger, lies, stealing, covetousness, etc. The child at this age is unsure of what is right or wrong and will most probably ask many questions (usually one question leads to another and another…). As a mentor, you must be available to watch and help your child grow (nothing else is more important than this). If you are not available, you stand the risk of your child taking up the character of whomever is available for them (that is what upbringing is all about) and you may accidentally have altered the destiny of your child!

Boring things like not wanting to share his toys, fighting siblings (normal but should be checked so it does not go overboard), lying about who took the biscuit from the carton, wanting to have his way all the time are red alerts to watch out for. At this point in the life of a child both male and female, the body begins to change. You have a lot of explaining to do, as the breast will begin to sprout and the menstrual cycle may begin in the case of a female child, public and underarm hairs emerge both in male and female. As a mentor, you must teach hygiene (you may buy anti-perspirant), understanding of the body changes, awareness of the opposite sex and effects the opposite sex will have and how to control such effects and also the consequences of very close/sexual interactions with the opposite sex. Statistics show that most children nowadays have their first sexual relationship before the age of 12!

When having a one on one talk with your child, the idea is not to be too graphic, but to be clear and not speak with ambiguity. Make sure that your child understands perfectly what you are saying and be ready to answer questions. A good way is to ask the Holy Spirit to help you. As a mentor, you must not be shy or ignore the situation thinking it will go away. It will not! You as a mentor must own up to your responsibility and that is to train up your child the way he should go (Prov. 22:6).

These are the teenage years. This is usually a very turbulent period in the life of a growing child. A teenager believes that he is no longer a child and should not be treated as one. The teenager at this stage does not seem to fit in any category. He is not a child but is also not an adult. Somehow, no one (except

fellow teenagers of course) understands him. It also does not help matters that a mentor watching his young child evolving into a young adult does not handle the transformation well and will make every attempt to suppress the changes reflected by the teenager. Please note that the more a mentor resists these changes, the more resolute, rebellious and withdrawn the teenager is. This period is definitely a very difficult one in the life of both the mentor and the teenager as it is the period they are most likely to lose the teenager to peer pressure. I will advise you to kindly follow these guidelines on your teenage child's discipline:

- ✓ Try to understand your teenager and the rationale behind his actions.
- ✓ Never condemn as you will only make him hide things from you. By the time you know, it might just be too late.
- ✓ Grow with your teenager; the only constant thing is change. If your teenager believes you are backwards, archaic, he will stop following your advice more often.
- ✓ Do not start too late. You should have been actively involved in training your child from birth otherwise it is too late to do so as a teenager. The character is already formed (it is only the grace of God that can help you at this point).
- ✓ Teach your teenage child all things they need to know about sex and life issues. If they learn the wrong things outside your home and make a mistake while exercising

their wrongly found knowledge, you will never see them coming back to you for correction. Do you know why; because they didn't learn it initially from you? They know they have done the wrong things and letting you know about it, is another disaster. With so much fear, they will go back to their wrong adviser who will confuse them the more. So patiently and prayerfully answer all their questions. Ignoring their questions will make them seek answers from their peers.

- ✓ Teenage stage of life is the period of choices that can make or mar their life. Pastor Gbile Akanni said that "these are choices that will mark their life out for greatness and glory or that will predispose them to perpetual defeat and failure. The unfortunate thing about these choices is that whether they were made consciously or unconsciously, they are often irreversible."
- ✓ Be honest and open with your teenager when talking about your values, beliefs and ideas. It may be wise to just say, "Here is what I think about….,"briefly explain your views by discussing the options they choose.
- ✓ If your teenager confides in you, do not tell everyone otherwise, you will never hear a thing from him anymore.

- ✓ Show love, acceptance. Most teenagers who fall into the wrong hands do so out of a quest for love and acceptance.
- ✓ Above all, you have to constantly lift up your teenage child in prayers. Prayers that will make him to have the confidence and conviction not to act according to how "wrongly everybody else does", even if he is the only one not acting that way. Pray against destiny changers. It is around this period that teenagers encounter unwanted pregnancies, drugs, uncompleted education etc.
- ✓ Define what it means to be a Christ's follower. Make them to understand that they must be saved from sin before they can qualify as followers of Christ. Lead them to Christ for genuine conversion and transformation.

At the age of 20 – 25 years, this is the time in the life of a young adult, a mentor should help prepare the young adult into being independent (on their own). A mentor should offer advice on guidelines to watch for in choosing a life partner. As a mentor, you can bring in your life experiences (good or bad) to counsel your child on the virtues to watch out for in choosing a partner. Note, however, that your years may be quite different from theirs. You should find out who your child is dating and encourage him to bring the person home. If for any reason you are going to object, it must be on a valid, unarguable point. Having a "feeling" that he will not make a good partner is not just good enough and this may harden your child's resolve to stay with the individual.

Sex Education

> "... Now the body is not for fornication but for the Lord; and the Lord for the body" (1 Corinthians 6:13).

It is never too early to teach a child to be aware of his body, the effect he/she may have on others as well as the consequences of acting on the wrong advice. As early as a child can talk, and understand words, he should be told not to allow anyone touch him/her "down there". Occasional checks should be done to give a mentor the assurance that he/she has not been touched "down there" by anyone. It is recommended that if it is a "girl child" the mother or a woman should be the one to give the "talk" and vice versa for a boy child.

At their formative stage, telling the child not to allow anyone to touch him/her and letting you know at once if it happens is a good way to start. Explain how God made boys and girls differently and they must not touch each other unless they are married. At the time the child goes to the higher institution and may have to interact more with the opposite sex, "the girl child" must have already began to sprout breast, start her menstrual cycle and develop hair around the body while the "boy child" also must have begun to exhibit manly traits. You may at this time go further by telling them what the consequences of their actions will be.

Encourage your child to tell you if he/she fancies anyone or vice versa. The truth of the matter is that it will happen, so the earlier we face the realities as mentors to avoid uncomfortable situations, the better for all concerned. We have at various stages in our lives had crushes on people that if we met them now we would wonder why however at that point in time, we could not help it. With your knowledge as the mentor, you will be the perfect person to help your child through these stages (as you know there will be many of them). This is the time to get down to basics. It is recommended that sometime around this period, you will have a refresher sex education "talk" with your young adult but this time armed with all types of birth control you can lay your hands on. I hope that it is done early enough before he/she might have seen/used them either in school or with friends. You will let your child know that though you are not in any way endorsing the use, you however will like your child not to act in ignorance and make mistake based on false teachings. Let him/her be aware that the consequences are not only unwanted pregnancies but also deadly diseases like HIV and a great sin against GOD.

Soft Etiquette:

A mentor must teach his child social, personal, dining and cultural etiquette. Training of a child is a lot of work and efforts should be made to make your child a better person than you were. If you were not taught any of these by your own mentors, that is an error that should be corrected and not transferred to your children. It is not an inheritance! Mentors should read up books, search the internet and confirm with the word of God the acceptable and decent way of living. These are the things that will help them to make important decisions in their lives which will transport them to positions of authority or greatness.

What to Teach a Girl Child:

Social etiquette

- ✓ How to seat properly – her thighs firmly together.
- ✓ Not to expose parts of her body in public.
- ✓ How to comport herself as a lady.
- ✓ Submission.
- ✓ Respect for men and the elderly.

Personal hygiene

- ✓ Clean undergarment
- ✓ Private menstrual period. When the time comes, there should be no smell.
- ✓ No underarm hair.

Dinning etiquette

- ✓ Eat with the mouth closed.
- ✓ No noise from the mouth when eating.
- ✓ Eat decently and moderately.
- ✓ No scraping of plate.
- ✓ How to use a set of cutlery.
- ✓ No piling up of plate in public.
- ✓ Cover the mouth to use the toothpick.

What to Teach a Boy Child:

Social etiquette

- ✓ How to be responsible.
- ✓ Manly roles.
- ✓ How to speak to and treat a girl.
- ✓ Respect for women and the elderly.

Personal hygiene

- ✓ To keep clean and not wear a pair of boxers for a week just because "it doesn't smell".
- ✓ How to keep sweat away.
- ✓ How to dress smartly and decently.

Dinning etiquette

- ✓ Eat with the mouth closed.
- ✓ No noise from the mouth when eating.
- ✓ Eat decently and moderately.
- ✓ No scraping of plate.
- ✓ How to use a set of cutlery.
- ✓ No piling up of plate in public.
- ✓ Cover the mouth to use the toothpick.

INSTILLING GODLY VALUES

What a child becomes in life is dependent on the type of training he receives. A child can be likened to a sponge; ready to soak up whatsoever they see along the way. The following are seven ways that can easily influence a child.

1. **School:**

The school a child attends has a great influence on the type of person such a child will become. Teachers are seen as role models and a child will often make statements like "my teacher said". Apart from educational aspect, a mentor should find out what values a school gives as well as what they deem important and what they regard as not important.

2. **Television / films / Pictures:**

As a mentor, it is your duty to know exactly what type of programs your children are allowed to watch. Children are imitators; they keep in their memory 70% of the movies/pictures they viewed. Letting a child know that some programs are not for children but adults is a start. This will quicken in their spirit if such programs come up when you are not at home. Most movies these days are rated in different categories so you may tell them to check that children can watch before they can watch. Great percentage of corruption in the society today comes from what the children watched in movies. What they watch is what they learn to practice. Even some mentors usually allow their children to watch movies that have been rated above the age of their child. This is wrong and must be stopped.

3. **Friends:**

Find out who your child's friend is. Discuss with him occasionally what they talk about. This will give you an insight into what upbringing such a friend has. Making statements like "my father has the latest / biggest car/ house" is not acceptable. Make friends with your child's friend's mentor (a good way to meet is in school or at children's parties) and determine if that is the type of person you will want your child to associate with. There is an adage that says "show me your friend and I will tell you who you are", bad companies' corrupt good manners and there can never be any relationship between light and darkness.

4. Church:

A good way of deciding if a church is good for you is to determine if there is a vibrant children's section. Find out what values they preach and determine if it is a good environment to bring up a child.

5. Social Networks/ Internet / Computer:

Watch out for the various web sites your child visits on the internet especially with their phone which is now highly connected to the internet. Do not encourage chat mates/rooms as statistics has shown that this plays a huge negative influence on a child. It is hard enough to read and understand a person you can see so someone you have never seen should never be encouraged. Searching of pornographic pictures and videos on the phone should be discouraged. As a discipline, you can give your child a manual phone until he proves his maturity in handling the internet connected phone.

6. **Neighbours:**

Watch out for whom your child plays with around the neighbourhood. Do not just allow your children to go into anybody's home. Discourage a child from house hopping. A child should understand the importance of staying in his house.

7. **Story Books / Novels**

Guide a child in determining the type of books he reads. Most books have an age range written on them so it is easy for you to pick out the type of books okay for your child's age group.

All of these will give conflicting views about life and it is your duty as a mentor to instill Godly values. The word of God is a reference point for us to determine right from wrong and understand what the will of God is.

Tool of Discipline

How does God expect us to discipline our children? He expects us to do it with the "rod". The rod is the tool of discipline. It must be used to mould the character and give shape to the life of our children.

The issue of discipline with the rod /stick/cane, etc, continues to be one of great debate in different cultures and homes. Some believe it is the proper thing to discipline a child with the rod while others believe it is child abuse and such a mentor should be locked up for using rod on his own child. The ideal thing to do is

to find out what the word of God says about this. The word of God instructs us that:

> **"Foolishness is bound in the heart of a child; but the rod of correction shall drive it far from him (Proverbs 22:15)".**

> "He that spareth his rod hateth his son: but he that loveth him chasteneth him quickly (Proverbs 13:24)".

> "Withhold not correction from the child: for if thou beatest him with the rod, he shall not die. Thou shalt beat him with the rod, and shalt deliver his soul from hell (Proverbs 23:13-14)".

> "The rod and reproof give wisdom: but a child left to himself bringeth his mother to shame (Proverbs 29:15)".

Scripturally, there are two types of "rod" – the spiritual and the physical.

The Spiritual Rod:

Isaiah 11:1-4 has this to say: "And there shall come forth a rod out of the stem of Jesse, and a branch shall grow out of his roots: …" The rod being referred to here is clearly Jesus Christ. Jesus Christ is also the word of God (John 1:1-14).

Again Revelation 19:13 says: "And he was clothed with a vesture dipped in blood: and his name is called the word of God." The spiritual rod is the word of God. It is the strongest rod you can use in disciplining your child. It has the inbuilt capability to change and transform the life of your child more than any physical cane can. Only the word of God can reach into the soul and spirit of a man, penetrating deep into places where a physical rod cannot go (Hebrews 4:12). What a tool for discipline!

I want to challenge all mentors to use more of the spiritual rod than the physical, it has a more lasting effect.

The Physical Rod:

The physical rod is the cane. There's an adage that says, "Spare the rod and spoil the child". This has some truth to it, particularly when you understand the rod to mean both the word of God and the physical rod. Never form a habit of **ALWAYS** beating your child with a cane, or else the child becomes hardened. It may, however, become necessary to reprove a child with a cane, once in a while.

If you have to beat your children, make sure you explain to him the reasons for your actions. Make sure he knows that love is behind it; otherwise they mistake your action to be hatred.

In cultures where the rod of disciplining is withheld, they are reaping the fruits of their lack of wisdom. Drugs, teenage parenthood, suicidal and psychopathic behaviour rule the day. There is disintegration in the land. If you as a mentor desire that your child brings you peace, joy and fulfillment, you will have to use the rod as a necessary tool in discipline. It is instructive to note that the use of the rod is not to inflict pain, rather it is to correct. Therefore, as mentors, we should not channel our energy toward getting a bigger and better cane but to find out ways we can get the child to understand the reason for the caning.

As a mentor, pay particular attention to the following summaries:

- ✓ Effective discipline is good for both you and the child. It will surely give you peace. Always remember that Eli the priest did not chastise his children and the priesthood was taken away from him.
- ✓ The ultimate goal is to correct your child and teach him how to behave, not to make him suffer.
- ✓ Teach by example. If you tell lies in the presence of your children, you cannot discipline such a child for lying or any other bad behaviour.
- ✓ The child must understand the reason for the discipline. As a mentor, you have to explain what exactly the child did wrong.
- ✓ Try not to use the cane too often otherwise, the child may develop a thick skin and it will diminish the effect of the discipline by the cane.
- ✓ You should listen to your child's explanations before proceeding to use the cane; he may have a valid reason for the action.

- ✓ If you go ahead to cane without listening, the purpose will be lost as he will rather feel cheated or wrongly treated.
- ✓ You should use words that will build self-esteem and confidence otherwise a child can have the feeling that he can never do anything right in your eyes.
- ✓ Resist the urge to use your hand or any part of your body to discipline your child. Two fingers on a child under one year old does not really matter as they can easily be made calm when they cry during discipline. However, slapping or kicking any child is not encouraged as the child may see it from the angle that the mentor hates him. You must separate the punishment from the punisher.

6
THE CLARION CALL

> *Do not train a child to learn by force or harshness; but direct them to it by what amuses their minds, so that you may be better able to discover with accuracy the peculiar bent of the genius of each.*
>
> - *Plato*

The training of children should be characterized by the same standard of moral excellence regardless of their personality, temperament, or gender. We do not lower the standards for the child but bring the child to the standard. Many mentors are guilty of dismissing the need for virtuous training based on their child's peculiarity. They will say to me, oh, but my child is different: the 'oh, but my child is different; is not a legitimate exception clause in the ethical scheme of the Bible.

I have recognized that all children are different. Brothers and sisters can be as different from each other as the child next door. Every child has a unique temperament and personality combination that distinguishes him from all others. However, personality development and moral training are not the same activities.

Personality is like the various sizes and styles of homes offered by a single contractor. Moral training is the consistent standard of training found in each home regardless of style. Regardless of the personality distinctions found in your children, persistent moral training should not be different from child to child because scripture's requirements for moral training are the same.

Your children all represent different personality types. But which personality type does the Bible exempt from demonstrating kindness, patience, self-control, gentleness, humility, endurance, obedience, respect, honesty, integrity, or other virtues? None, of course. I, strongly encourage mentors to recognize and appreciate the uniqueness of each child, but understand that uniqueness does not change the standard of ethical training. Temperaments, personalities, and even gender cannot be used to excuse wrong. The virtues and values of life are the same for all and apply to all ages regardless of gender or temperament. The duty of mentors is to continually bring their children to God's standard and not lower the standard to suit the child.

Set the standard for acceptable behaviours in the home, in the neighbourhood, at school, in church, among strangers, etc. the standards you set for your children should be to guide them, not to choke or clog them. Children within the age brackets of 3 – 10 years are often very adventurous. They want to explore possibilities. They want to explore the world around them. Ensure that the standards you set are not such that limit, intimidate or make them feel less human and unloved.

Make set standards clear enough. Map out clearly what standards of proper behaviour you want your child to maintain. It is best to discuss these standards with him, and be sure he clearly understands what is required of him. Making standard's and limits clear enough is important, so that when punishment has to be meted out for disobedience, it won't seem unfair to the child. Yes, when you discipline a child for an instruction he didn't clearly understand, he may feel it's a deliberate attempt to make him suffer for nothing. Be mindful of this.

The Role of God's Grace

Grace is God's ability and strength working in men to achieve tremendous result beyond natural human's ability. God said in his word "be strong in the grace that is in Christ Jesus (2 Timothy 2:1). Only by the Grace of God can the task of training God's children be achieved. The duty of Christian mentors to instruct their children in the knowledge of God cannot be achieved apart from His grace.

As a mentor, you want many things for your child. But the most important issue must be your child's salvation. You may wonder what you can do to influence your child's decision. Isn't salvation a personal issue? You ask. "I certainly don't have the power to make it happen". This is true. Salvation occurs, as the Bible says, by grace alone, through faith alone (Ephesians 2:8-9). Yet, many mentors wrongly conclude that dependence upon grace means they should give up all responsibility or let go and let God. The belief follows this logic: why should parents bother to develop the moral character and conduct of their children if grace and salvation, the supreme goals, are not the direct result of moral training? As the Bible states;

> **"Therefore by the deeds of the law there shall no flesh be justified in his sight:... (Romans 3:20).**

The simplest answer to that question is that God requires the training of children. Proverbs 22:6 calls for us to "Train a child in the way he should go, "what is the result? "and when he is old, he will not depart from it". Ephesians 6:1-3 promises, "children, obey your parents in the Lord: for this is right. Honour thy father and mother; which is the first commandment with promise, that it may be well with thee, and thou mayest live long on the earth.

Mentors should participate in the communication of God's grace by opening the child's mind to, and directing his ways in God's moral law. In this way, children are brought to knowledge of God. Mentors need to cooperate with the grace of God. A biblical view of grace doesn't call for parents to labour less. Rather, it calls them to labour fervently, all the while acknowledging their utter dependency upon God.

Seek diligently the salvation of your child that he might enter into the fullness of God's power and influence and, out of a love response to God, serve Him wholeheartedly. In training God's children, grace and labour are not enemies but divinely appointed comrades in the work of the Lord. You cannot train children by your own strength and still achieve a godly outcome. Remember; let God through his grace do His work, while you through obedience do yours.

Feed my Lambs

We are the shepherd of our children, to lead them through unknown and uncharted paths of life. Jesus as He departed to heaven asked Peter three times in John 21:15-16. Do you love me, then feed my sheep. But note that the first time Jesus asked the question he told Peter to feed my lamb. Later he said feed my sheep. The lamb is the child of the sheep. We must nurture and feed our children as a demonstration of our love for Jesus Christ. We must nurture them with the word of God. If we are to do that then we must follow what God said to Joshua:

> **"This book of the law shall not depart out of thy mouth; but thou shalt mediate therein day and night, that thou mayest observe to do according to all that is written therein: for then thou shalt make thy way prosperous, and then thou shalt have good success. (Joshua 1:8)**

When we do that we can confidently say that as for me and my house, we will serve the LORD (Joshua 24:15).

Effect of Prayer

Above all, we can never underestimate the life-changing effect of prayer. In prayer, you wield control over the physical realm. On the other hand, praying for your children will help them walk in God's plan for their lives. As a mentor, speak into the life of your child. Proclaim the word of God into his life with every opportunity. Do not ever curse your child. If he is not too good in school or a subject, get a teacher to support in that area. Making statements like "he is not good in mathematics", she cannot speak good English" is not acceptable. Call things that are not as though they were and prayerfully address the situation and you will begin to see results. Every morning and opportunity, speak into the life of your child:

- ✓ You will not die but live.
- ✓ You will prosper, in your generation you will matter.
- ✓ You will excel in all areas of your life.
- ✓ The Lord will never leave you nor forsake you.
- ✓ Whatever you lay your hands to do will prosper.
- ✓ You will make me proud.
- ✓ You are the best in your school and it's only you can make it right.
- ✓ You are for signs and wonders.
- ✓ You are born to win and reign in life.
- ✓ You are not an ordinary person.
- ✓ You are destined for greatness, etc.

In conclusion, I want you to understand that it takes being a child of God for you to truly comprehend and understand this "Clarion call". If you are a mentor, and you are not yet born again and you would like to, please pray this simple prayer with sincerity:

> "Dear Father, I come to you today. I am a sinner. Forgive me my sins. I am sorry for all my wrong doings. I believe that Jesus Christ died for me and was raised on the third day for the remission of my sins, Forgive me Oh Lord. Cleanse me with the precious Blood of Jesus Christ. I accept Jesus today as my Lord and Saviour. Thank you Father, for now I know, that I am born again. Fill me with your spirit and direct me in all my ways. All these I pray in the name of Jesus Christ. Amen.

IN CONCLUSION

Your Child's Time-Table

"Have you anything to say before I sentence you?" A Canadian judge asked the seventeen-year –old youth, who had committed murder and who, himself, was soon to hear the death sentence pronounced. "Yes, Your Honour, I have something to say," he replied shyly. "Am I alone responsible for the crime I committed? My father put the first bottle of alcohol in my hand. My parents taught me that there is nothing to religion. I never saw a Bible in my home. I never heard my parents pray. May God have mercy on their souls and mine?"

What a wasted life! In this story, the teenage boy pointed out areas of neglect by his mentors that led to his delinquency. The bible says, ***"Train up a child in the way he should go: and when he is old he will not depart from it"*** (Proverbs 22:6). As Christian parent, there are guidelines and tips for training your child; using a workable time-table is part of the guidelines.

The time –table for your child's training must be all-inclusive for his total character formation. A time-table is a plan showing times of events, e.g. routine at home. The effective use of a time-table will enable your child to be responsible and helpful to people around him. By it, your child's activities can be planned and determined; the child is also put under control. The earlier your child gets accustomed to predetermined routines at home, the easier it becomes for him to adapt to routines at school. When the time-table is initially introduced, it may be confronted with opposition, but after continuous use for two weeks your child will adjust. It will amaze you how he will keep up with time.

I believe that as you prayerfully identify the areas of neglect as pointed out by the boy in the opening illustration, you will be able to draw a balanced time-table that will be all-encompassing, taking into consideration the physical, social, intellectual, emotional and spiritual development of your child at various stages.

The different developmental stages of each child will help to determine the right time and duration of each activity in the time-table. You need to understand that not two days are ever really the same; there are days for services and other church activities, vacation, etc. it is good to make a list of things that are essential for the day to day development of a child, including things that can crop up to change the day's activities.

Essential Parts of a Time-Table

- ✓ You must understand that the most important thing in the character development of your child is the spiritual. This must be given a significant place and time in the time-table.

- ✓ His physical, social, intellectual and emotional development is also very important and should be well attended to.

- ✓ Let him have opportunity to learn hard work by helping with household chores.

- ✓ Waking him early enough to participate in family devotion will help in preparing him for personal quiet time when he is old enough to do so. He will also have the understanding that a family must pray together to stay together.

- ✓ Give time to private studies by putting such a time when you will be available to assist with home-work, and reading of other good books.

- ✓ Make Bible reading time an interesting and a must do thing, ensuring that the time and duration are right. You can share the reading together by reading alternate verses.

- ✓ Give time to preparatory for school. It is best done as the last thing before the child goes to bed. Get the bag for books packed while the lunch box is in place for what will be put in it the following day. Keep uniform, shoes and socks where they can be easily reached.

- ✓ Meal times must be such that you have at least a meal together as a family, and allow the child assist in the preparation of meals.

- ✓ There must be time for siesta and recreation, for "all work and no play make Jack a dull boy."

- ✓ Include prayer time in his time-table, and be there to assist him. The place, time and duration of prayer must also be determined. Make it an interesting time.

- ✓ It is good to involve the child in the preparation of the time-table, and there should be room for adjustment as the need arises.

- ✓ The time-table should be made beautifully with colours.

As you do all you can to bring the best out of your child, train him to be who God actually wants him to be, your child training efforts will be richly rewarded in Jesus name!

ABOUT THE AUTHOR

Stanley Ifeanyi Kalu, for more than a decade, has been part of the on-going charismatic revival in the Presbyterian Children Ministry (PCM), and the Children Evangelism Ministry (C.E.M) under the Presbyterian Church of Nigeria.

Today, he teaches the children section and teenage class of St. Andrews Presbyterian Church of Nigeria, First Aba Parish, with over 600 children and teenagers in attendance. Stanley is a lieutenant in the Boy's Brigade Nigeria, 4th Aba Company under the Aba Battalion Council where he helps to instill discipline, promote the habit of obedience and guide the boys towards Christ kingdom.

Stanley has attended over 20 children ministry training and workshops. He has taught extensively in many organizations. He has counseled many teenagers through their battles and period of choices. Stanley is a professional Civil Engineer, a children teacher, speaker, author, and a writer. He is highly enthusiastic about this book.

ENDNOTES

The editions below were those used in researching the book. Original publication dates are stated in each of the 5 commentaries. Works freely available on the internet are preceded by an asterisk. Before downloading or using them you should check if they are legally in the public domain in the country where you live.

> Gbile Akanni (April 2013), Battle for the Young, Peace House Publication, Gboko, Benue State.

> Changing Boundaries (August 2013), Christian Women Mirror Magazine. Life Press Limited Publication, Vol. 20 No. 10

> *Jeffrey Fall, "Successful Parenting: God's Way" in Tomorrow's World. Available at http://www.tomorrowsworld.org/booklets/successful-parenting-gods-way

*Oyewale Tomori, (March, 2007), Mentoring God's Heritage, presented at the 8th Redeemer's Day of the Christ the Redeemer's School Movement, Redeemer's University. Available at www.run.edu.ng/downloads/MENTORING%20GOD%27S%20HERITAGE.doc

*Practical Living, Practical Christian Living Initiative. Available at www.pclng.org

Please visit our website: www.childrenmentorsinc.com.ng
to review:

- ✓ Additional Information about Children Mentoring products.

- ✓ Frequent Asked Questions (FAQ) about our trainings.

- ✓ Children Mentors Inc.'s events.

- ✓ Weekly inspiration from Children Mentors Inc.

- ✓ And much more

If you want to order books or have any request, feel free to contact the author on:

E-mail: childrenmentorsinc@gmail.com
Tel: +234 803 7024 964

Or

Write to:

Stanley Ifeanyi Kalu
The Presbyterian Children Ministry
St Andrews Presbyterian Church of Nigeria
First Aba Parish
1 Azikiwe Road,
P. O. Box 493,
Aba - Abia State, Nigeria

www.ingramcontent.com/pod-product-compliance
Lightning Source LLC
Chambersburg PA
CBHW071520040426
42444CB00008B/1736